A2
KEY
FOR SCHOOLS 1

WITHOUT ANSWERS

AUTHENTIC PRACTICE TESTS

Cambridge University Press
www.cambridge.org/elt

Cambridge Assessment English
www.cambridgeenglish.org

Information on this title: www.cambridge.org/9781108718325

© Cambridge University Press & Assessment and UCLES 2019

First published 2019

20 19 18 17 16

Printed in Great Britain by Ashford Colour Press Ltd.

A catalogue record for this publication is available from the British Library

ISBN 978-1-108-67659-5 A2 Key for Schools 1 Student's Book with answers with Audio
ISBN 978-1-108-71832-5 A2 Key for Schools 1 Student's Book without answers
ISBN 978-1-108-71833-2 A2 Key for Schools 1 Audio CDs (2)

Contents

Introduction

This collection of four complete practice tests contains papers from the *Cambridge English Qualifications A2 Key for Schools* examination. Students can practise these tests on their own or with the help of a teacher.

The *A2 Key for Schools* examination is part of a series of Cambridge English Qualifications for general and higher education. This series consists of five qualifications that have similar characteristics but are designed for different levels of English language ability. The *A2 Key for Schools* certificate is recognised around the world as a basic qualification in English.

Cambridge English Qualifications	CEFR Level	UK National Qualifications Framework Level
C2 Proficiency	C2	3
C1 Advanced	C1	2
B2 First for Schools	B2	1
B1 Preliminary for Schools	B1	Entry 3
A2 Key for Schools	A2	Entry 2

Further information

The information contained in this practice book is designed to be an overview of the exam. For a full description of all of the above exams, including information about task types, testing focus and preparation, please see the relevant handbooks which can be obtained from the Cambridge Assessment English website at: **cambridgeenglish.org**.

The structure of *A2 Key for Schools*: an overview

The *Cambridge English Qualifications A2 Key for Schools* examination consists of three papers:

Reading and Writing: 60 minutes

Candidates need to be able to understand simple written information such as signs and newspapers, and produce simple written English.

Listening: 30 minutes approximately

Candidates need to show they can follow and understand a range of spoken materials such as announcements, when people speak reasonably slowly.

Speaking: 8–10 minutes

Candidates take the Speaking test with another candidate or in a group of three. They are tested on their ability to take part in different types of interaction: with the examiner, with the other candidate and by themselves.

	Overall length	Number of tasks/ parts	Number of items
Reading and Writing	60 mins	7	32
Listening	approx. 30 mins	5	25
Speaking	8–10 mins	2	–
Total	approx. 1 hour 40 mins		

Grading

All candidates receive a Statement of Results and candidates whose performance ranges between CEFR Levels A1 and B1 (Cambridge English Scale scores of 100–150) also receive a certificate.

- Candidates who achieve **Grade A** (Cambridge English Scale scores of 140–150) receive the Key for Schools English Test certificate stating that they demonstrated ability at Level B1.
- Candidates who achieve **Grade B** or **C** (Cambridge English Scale scores of 120–139) receive the Key for Schools English Test certificate at Level A2.
- Candidates whose performance is below A2 level, but falls within **Level A1** (Cambridge English Scale scores of 100–119), receive a Cambridge English certificate stating that they have demonstrated ability at Level A1.

For further information on grading and results, go to the website (see page 5 for details).

Speaking: an overview for candidates

The Speaking test lasts 8–10 minutes. You will take the test with another candidate. There are two examiners but only one of them will talk to you. The examiner will ask you questions and ask you to talk to the other candidate.

Part 1 (3–4 minutes)
The examiner will ask you and your partner some questions. These questions will be about your daily life, interests, likes and dislikes. For example, you may have to speak about school, hobbies or home town.

Part 2 (5–6 minutes)
You and your partner will speak to each other. The examiner will give you a card with some illustrations on it. You will then discuss the activities, things or places illustrated on the card with your partner. The examiner will then ask you and your partner some individual questions about the illustrations on the card.

Test 1

READING AND WRITING (60 minutes)

PART 1

QUESTIONS 1–6

For each question, choose the correct answer.

1

Found: blue sports bag

Collect from school office
(with student ID card)

A A student has found the wrong ID card in his sports bag.

B The person who lost his bag can get it from the school office.

C If you find a lost sports bag, please take it to the school office.

2

Room 3.1
Mrs Gray's students

This room is closed
for repairs. Lessons in
room 4.2 until Friday

A Mrs Gray is not coming to the school until Friday.

B Mrs Gray's class is going to be on a different day this week.

C Mrs Gray isn't able to use her usual room at the moment.

3

File Edit Tools View Message Help

From: Head teacher

To: All students

The school kitchen will be closed for hot lunches Monday – Friday next week. We can still serve sandwiches and salads.

A Students have to bring their own food to school for lunch next week.

B The school is going to stop offering lunch to students after next week.

C Only a few types of food will be available for student lunches next week.

4

Hi Suzy,
I've finished our history project. Shall I bring it round later to show you before I give it to the teacher tomorrow?
Mark

A   Mark is asking Suzy if he should visit her today.

B   Mark wants Suzy to help him complete their project.

C   Mark thinks Suzy should give the project to the teacher.

5

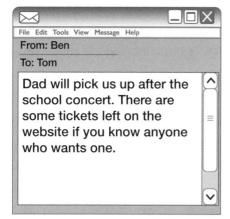

From: Ben
To: Tom

Dad will pick us up after the school concert. There are some tickets left on the website if you know anyone who wants one.

What should Tom do?

A   go online to check if there are still concert tickets available

B   tell people that it is still possible for them to come to the concert

C   ask if his father can collect them after the concert

6

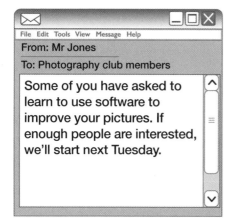

From: Mr Jones
To: Photography club members

Some of you have asked to learn to use software to improve your pictures. If enough people are interested, we'll start next Tuesday.

A   Mr Jones is offering to teach club members something new.

B   Some people have told Mr Jones they want to leave the photography club.

C   Mr Jones wants to find out more about photography software.

PART 2

QUESTIONS 7–13

For each question, choose the correct answer.

		Jian	Max	Kojo
7	Who does not like the way the book ends?	A	B	C
8	Who enjoyed the pictures in the book?	A	B	C
9	Who explains how he got the book?	A	B	C
10	Who enjoyed learning about lives which are different from his own?	A	B	C
11	Who says something about what happens in the story?	A	B	C
12	Who says the book is not very well-known?	A	B	C
13	Who felt sad when he finished the book?	A	B	C

My favourite book

Jian

This well-known book was in a box of old books that a neighbour gave me. I wasn't sure about it when I picked it up because I saw the pictures and thought it was a book for little children. But I was bored, so I started reading. After a few pages I couldn't stop, and when I got to the last page, I was quite upset that there wasn't more. It's about two friends who play a game, and how it changes their lives. It's brilliant!

Max

This was one of the first books I ever had, but it's still a favourite. Even before I could read, I loved looking at the drawings as my parents read the story to me. Now my little sister's got it, and she loves it too. The writer has become quite famous, but this is the first book she wrote, and not many people have heard of it. It's very different from the books she wrote later. I suppose what you write about changes as your life changes.

Kojo

I read this book for the first time when I was about eight. One of the reasons I liked it was that it was about people growing up in a place which I knew nothing about. My friend read it too, and our ideas for games often came from this book. I read it again recently, and I still think it's great, except the last few pages. What happens in them doesn't seem real.

PART 3

QUESTIONS 14–18

For each question, choose the correct answer.

A young cheesemaker

16-year-old Pat Tulloch has an unusual hobby. She makes cheese on the family farm in Australia. She began by making yoghurt with her mother when she was little. Then she started watching her father's workers make cheese. When she was ten, she made some herself for the first time. 'It wasn't great,' she says, 'but the workers told me what I was doing wrong and that helped me to slowly get better.'

Pat always needs good milk for her cheese, but she doesn't have to buy it. Her mother and father keep 100 cows on their farm. Pat can just ask them when she needs more. Last year, Pat's neighbour gave her a young cow to keep and look after, but it doesn't produce milk to make cheese yet.

Pat and her family make several types of cheese. Recently they won a prize for one of them. 'It's been great for helping customers find out about us,' says Pat. 'Last month we started selling cheese in New Zealand. People there read about our prize in a food magazine. Soon we're going to do some advertisements, too.'

Pat's next idea is to post some online recipes for cooking with cheese. 'One of my favourites is cheese with eggs for breakfast. It's great! Our cheese is also lovely with pasta – I hope a restaurant might buy some one day.' But right now Pat is still at school. 'Making cheese is fun and winning a prize for it is great, but doing well in my studies matters more for now.'

---

14   Pat learned to make good cheese

    A   by listening to the advice she got.

    B   by seeing how her mother did it.

    C   by practising at home on her own.

15   Where does Pat get the milk for her cheese?

    A   from her neighbour's farm

    B   her father helps her to buy it

    C   her parents give it to her

16   Pat says winning the prize means

    A   more people know about her family's cheese.

    B   she can be the star of the family's new advertisements.

    C   she was invited to visit another country.

17   What's the most important thing for Pat at the moment?

    A   writing a new cookbook

    B   being successful at school

    C   selling cheese to a restaurant

18   In this article, Pat is explaining

    A   why her family started making cheese.

    B   how to win a competition for making cheese.

    C   how she has become part of a cheese-making business.

PART 4

QUESTIONS 19–24

For each question, choose the correct answer.

Philo T. Farnsworth

Philo T. Farnsworth was born in the USA in 1906. As a child, he was very interested in science and electricity and spent a lot of time **(19)** .... about it. He also won a national **(20)** .... for young engineers when he was just 13.

When he was 20, Farnsworth **(21)** .... his own business. In 1927, he showed everyone his new idea: a **(22)** .... of sending pictures using electricity. Many other people were working on ideas for a machine to do this, but Farnsworth's was the first that had no moving parts. In fact, it was the first true electronic TV.

After many business problems, Farnsworth had success in 1938 when another company **(23)** .... him $1 million for his idea. He is not very famous these **(24)** .... , but, as the father of electronic television, Farnsworth changed the world.

19	A learning	B studying	C understanding
20	A game	B match	C competition
21	A became	B turned	C started
22	A plan	B way	C thing
23	A offered	B took	C sold
24	A times	B days	C years

PART 5

QUESTIONS 25–30

For each question, write the correct answer.

Write **ONE** word for each gap.

Example:

0	*from*

From:	Rachel
To:	Chris

We're back **(0)** .... our family holiday in the US. It was amazing! It's **(25)** ....

biggest country I've ever been to. We travelled from Los Angeles to Seattle

(26) .... car. It's nearly 2000 km and the trip took us **(27)** .... very long

time – nearly a week.

My family liked Los Angeles best, **(28)** .... I didn't agree – Seattle was my favourite

place. It's smaller **(29)** .... Los Angeles, and the food was better. Seattle is near the

sea and we ate lots of fish. The only problem was that **(30)** .... rained almost

every day!

Let's meet for a chat soon. I have a present for you!

PART 6

QUESTION 31

You are going camping next weekend with your family.
Write an email to your English friend, Lee.

In your email:

- ask Lee to come camping with you and your family

- say why you are going camping

- tell Lee what to bring.

Write **25 words** or more.

Write the email on your answer sheet.

PART 7

QUESTION 32

Look at the three pictures.
Write the story shown in the pictures.
Write **35 words** or more.

Write the story on your answer sheet.

LISTENING (approximately 30 minutes)

PART 1

QUESTIONS 1–5

For each question, choose the correct answer.

---

1 How did Stan and his dad get home from the concert?

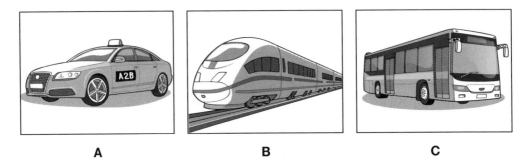

| A | B | C |

2 What's the girl forgotten?

| A | B | C |

3 What will the boy do first after he gets home from school?

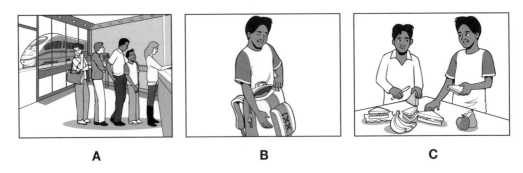

| A | B | C |

4   Where did the girl find her phone?

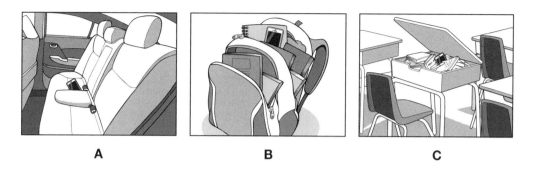

A   B   C

5   Where are the two friends going to go first today?

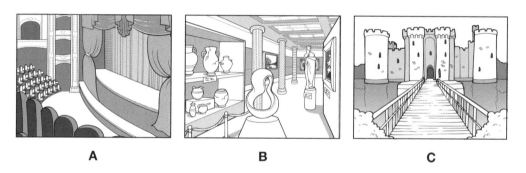

A   B   C

PART 2

QUESTIONS 6–10

For each question, write the correct answer in the gap. Write **one word** or a **number** or a **date** or a **time**.

You will hear a man talking about a course for teenagers who are interested in working on the radio.

Radio camp for teenagers

Address: 102 Golden Street

Date first course starts: (6) ....

Learn to write: (7) ....

Meet world famous: (8) ....

Each person receives: (9) ....

Discount price: (10) $.......................................

PART 3

QUESTIONS 11–15

For each question, choose the correct answer.

___

You will hear Edward talking to his friend Michaela about dance classes.

11   Where does Edward go for his dance classes?

    A   a college

    B   a dance school

    C   a sports centre

12   Michaela started going to classes

    A   one week ago.

    B   four weeks ago.

    C   eight weeks ago.

13   Why does Edward like his teacher?

    A   She's very funny.

    B   She gives students presents.

    C   She explains things clearly.

14   What does Michaela wear to her dance classes?

    A   trousers and a shirt

    B   shorts and a T-shirt

    C   trainers and a sweater

15   What does Edward enjoy most about the classes?

    A   learning new dances

    B   listening to the music

    C   meeting his friends

PART 4

QUESTIONS 16–20

For each question, choose the correct answer.

---

16   You will hear a brother and sister talking about a present for their cousin, Ben.
     Why did the girl choose the bag?

     A   It was the right price.

     B   It was the right size.

     C   It will be very useful.

17   You will hear a boy talking to a friend about a computer game.
     Why doesn't he buy it now?

     A   He's played it before.

     B   He thinks it's too expensive.

     C   He can borrow it from his friend.

18   You will hear two friends talking together.
     Where are they?

     A   at a farm

     B   in a forest

     C   on a mountain

19   You will hear a girl, Kate, talking to her father.
     What's Kate's father going to do?

     A   book a holiday

     B   enter a competition

     C   buy a magazine

20   You will hear two friends talking about last weekend.
     What did the boy do?

     A   He went shopping.

     B   He stayed at home.

     C   He visited a classmate.

PART 5

QUESTIONS 21–25

For each question, choose the correct answer.

You will hear Beth talking to Jack about a class trip.
What will each person bring on the trip?

Example:

0	Jack	B

People			**Things to bring**		
21	Edward	☐	A	board game
			B	camera
22	Beth	☐	C	drum
23	Dan	☐	D	guitar
			E	pencils and paints
24	Yolanda	☐	F	picnic bag
25	Gordon	☐	G	quiz
			H	sports equipment

You now have 6 minutes to write your answers on the answer sheet.

Test 2

READING AND WRITING (60 minutes)

PART 1

QUESTIONS 1–6

For each question, choose the correct answer.

1

Fashionista Clothes

Please keep the receipt –
you cannot return
anything without it.

A   Make sure that your receipt is correct before you leave the shop.

B   If you want to bring something back to this shop, you need a receipt.

C   Someone will check your receipt when you go out of the shop.

2

Luke,
Thanks for asking me to go to the cinema. It sounds fun, but I'm afraid I've got too much homework. Maybe some other time.
Sally

Sally is telling Luke

A   why she is too busy to see a movie.

B   which homework she needs to complete.

C   when she will be available to see a movie.

3

Did anyone pick up my biology textbook by mistake after our science lesson in the library? I don't mind coming to get it from you.
Jessica

A   Jessica needs to borrow a textbook from someone in her science class.

B   Jessica wants someone from her science class to bring her textbook to her.

C   Jessica is hoping someone in her science class has found her textbook.

4

Why did Nathan write the message?

A   to check if Laila can work on their art project over the weekend

B   to tell Laila he won't be able to complete the project on his own

C   to ask Laila if she's able to meet him earlier than they planned

5

24 hour sale!

Download any 10 songs for 99p

Then £1.99 per song as usual

A   You have 24 hours to buy as many songs as you like for 99p each.

B   The cost of each song is £1.99 after you buy more than ten songs.

C   Some popular songs that cost £1.99 aren't included in the sale.

6

A   Stella is checking when Aaron will need his bike back.

B   Stella can't say exactly when she will be able to return Aaron's bike.

C   Stella wants to know if she can borrow Aaron's bike until next weekend.

PART 2

QUESTIONS 7–13

For each question, choose the correct answer.

		DJ Fire	DJ Goldrock	DJ Mango
7	Who travels to different countries every year to play his music?	A	B	C
8	Who comes from a family of musicians?	A	B	C
9	Who was paid to make music as a teenager?	A	B	C
10	Who knows how to play more than one musical instrument?	A	B	C
11	Who works for a radio station?	A	B	C
12	Who writes music for other musicians?	A	B	C
13	Who wanted to play in a band when he was younger?	A	B	C

How three young people became DJs

DJ Fire

This Russian DJ grew up travelling with his parents who were in a rock band. He started learning piano at four, and drums at twelve. As a teenager, he wrote songs and posted them online as a hobby. Then, at 20, a music company started paying him to write songs for pop bands – and some have been on the radio. Later he became interested in electronic music and started playing it in clubs. He's hoping to get an invitation to play at some international festivals this summer.

DJ Goldrock

This South African DJ started playing the piano when he was 5. At 15, he played pop songs at a cousin's birthday party, and got a hundred kids dancing. At that moment, he knew he wanted to be a DJ and never have a normal job. He started a website where he played his favourite songs, and soon had lots of fans. He's now 20 and has his own show on national radio. For the past three years, he's spent his summers going around the world playing dance music at festivals.

DJ Mango

At 15, this Brazilian DJ's parents gave him a new computer and DJ equipment for making electronic dance music. Later that year, he started playing music at local dance parties to make some extra money, and the parties just got bigger and bigger. A few years later, a journalist asked him why he became a DJ. He said that as a child his dream was to play the electric guitar for a rock group, but he wasn't good enough!

PART 3

QUESTIONS 14–18

For each question, choose the correct answer.

A path across Canada

Thirteen-year-old Kara Finch writes about The Great Trail – a footpath that goes across Canada.

The Great Trail goes from one side of Canada to the other. At 24,000 km, it is the longest trail in the world. The Great Trail project began in 1992 and took 25 years to complete. It opened in 2017, exactly 150 years after Canada became one country.

The Great Trail is actually lots of paths joined together. You can cycle, walk or horse-ride on most of it, but there are parts where the only way you can travel is by boat. And there are others where the trail is part of the highway, which doesn't sound very safe to me.

My father and I spent a day walking along part of the Great Trail that was surprisingly busy. We were told you don't usually see bears when there are lots of people, but we did. It was moving through the trees, quite close to us, and I felt a little afraid. 'I don't think it's hungry!' laughed my dad.

At lunchtime, we talked to an old man on the trail. Dad asked him if he thought the path was going to help Canadians learn more about their countryside. 'Not really,' he said. 'We've always loved to be outdoors. But it will bring us tourists from around the world, which is important.'

In the future, the path will probably change, and new parts may open. We saw nothing to tell us we were on the Great Trail, which is a shame. I know there's information on the website, but it's good to know when you're walking on a special path. They need to add some signs, I think.

---

14   What is Kara doing in the first paragraph?

    A   telling tourists how long it takes to walk the Great Trail

    B   explaining the history of the Great Trail

    C   giving walkers advice about walking in Canada

15   What does Kara think is dangerous?

    A   Some parts of the path are on roads.

    B   You need a boat for parts of the path.

    C   Bikes and horses share the same path.

16   What does Kara say about the bear she saw?

    A   It looked hungry.

    B   It was on the path.

    C   It walked near her.

17   What did the old man say about the trail?

    A   People from other countries will come to see it.

    B   People will go into the countryside more because of it.

    C   People from Canada will use it to see other parts of their country.

18   What does Kara say should happen next?

    A   There should be a website about the trail.

    B   Some parts of the trail should close.

    C   There should be more signs along the trail.

PART 4

QUESTIONS 19–24

For each question, choose the correct answer.

Sally Ride

Sally Ride was born on 26th May, 1951, in California, USA. After high school, she went to Stanford University to study physics. While she was there, she saw an advertisement in her university newspaper **(19)** .... women to join the US space programme. Six women, including Sally, were **(20)** .... to become astronauts. On 18th June 1983, Sally became the first American woman to fly into space. Six days later, on 24th June, she **(21)** .... to Earth.

When Sally **(22)** .... working as an astronaut in 1987, she started teaching at the University of California. She wanted to find ways to get more people, **(23)** .... girls, interested in studying science and mathematics. She also found time to write science books for children about **(24)** .... space.

19	A	inviting	B	showing	C	looking
20	A	thought	B	decided	C	chosen
21	A	completed	B	returned	C	arrived
22	A	ended	B	closed	C	stopped
23	A	especially	B	exactly	C	clearly
24	A	exploring	B	going	C	travelling

PART 5

QUESTIONS 25–30

For each question, write the correct answer.
Write **ONE** word for each gap.

Example:

0	*got*

From:	Riley
To:	Kris

My dad's **(0)** .... three tickets for the hockey match next Wednesday. One was for

my brother, but now he's **(25)** .... free that day, so we have an extra one. Do you

(26) .... to come? Dad would like to leave our house at 4 o' clock. Let me know as soon

(27) .... possible.

From:	Kris
To:	Riley

Wow! That's really kind **(28)** .... you. Thanks! I asked Mum if I can come and she

said yes. I finish school a bit later **(29)** .... you, so Mum will drive me to your house

at 4 o'clock. Is there anything I need **(30)** .... bring with me?

PART 6

QUESTION 31

You would like to go to the cinema with your English friend, Andi.
Write an email to Andi.

In your email:

- ask Andi to go to the cinema with you

- say why you want to go to the cinema

- explain how you will travel there.

Write **25 words** or more.

Write the email on your answer sheet.

PART 7

QUESTION 32

Look at the three pictures.
Write the story shown in the pictures.
Write **35 words** or more.

Write the story on your answer sheet.

LISTENING (approximately 30 minutes)

PART 1

QUESTIONS 1–5

For each question, choose the correct answer.

---

1   Which photo is the boy showing his mother?

A   B   C

2   Where does the girl's mother work?

A   B   C

3   What did Helena's class do in their history lesson?

A   B   C

4 Which new sport is the girl going to do today?

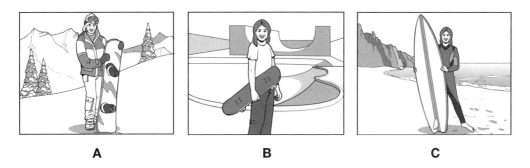

A   B   C

5 What did the boy eat for breakfast?

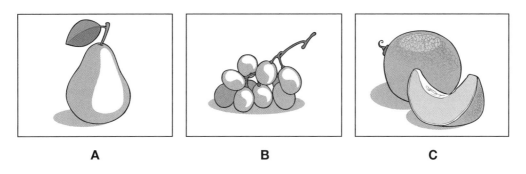

A   B   C

PART 2

QUESTIONS 6–10

For each question, write the correct answer in the gap. Write **one word** or a **number** or a **date** or a **time**.

You will hear a teacher telling a class about some homework.

Homework

Day to give to teacher:	Friday
Find out about:	(6) ....
Textbook page:	(7) ....
Website address:	(8) www. .... .com
Number of words to write:	(9) ....
Include:	(10) ....

PART 3

QUESTIONS 11–15

For each question, choose the correct answer.

You will hear Connie talking to her friend Tom about an activity club in the school holidays.

11 Connie thinks that the club is best for children aged

    A over 13.

    B from 11 to 13.

    C as young as 9.

12 What does Connie say about the club?

    A All the coaches are friendly.

    B The activities can be hard.

    C She knows everyone there.

13 Which activity is Tom interested in trying?

    A swimming

    B playing football

    C sailing

14 Connie says Tom needs to take

    A some money.

    B a towel.

    C his own lunch.

15 The shop that sells sports clothes is opposite

    A the cinema.

    B the hospital.

    C the bank.

PART 4

QUESTIONS 16–20

For each question, choose the correct answer.

---

16 You will hear two friends talking about going swimming together.
Why doesn't the girl want to go swimming?

A She's too busy.

B She feels ill.

C She's got no money.

17 You will hear two friends talking about a school trip.
Where are they going to go on the school trip?

A to a farm

B to a museum

C to a stadium

18 You will hear a teacher talking to his class.
What's he talking to them about?

A changes to their timetable

B a new teacher at the school

C a problem with a classroom

19 You will hear a boy, Oscar, talking about running.
How does Oscar feel now?

A tired

B bored

C worried

20 You will hear a boy, Alex, talking to a friend about a new T-shirt.
Why didn't Alex buy the blue and white T-shirt?

A It was the wrong size.

B It was too expensive.

C It was the wrong colour.

PART 5

QUESTIONS 21–25

For each question, choose the correct answer.

You will hear two friends, Luke and Claire, discussing plans for a school show.
Where will each person put a poster for the show?

Example:

| 0 | Luke | **E** |

People

21	Claire	☐
22	Paul	☐
23	James	☐
24	Joe	☐
25	Karen	☐

Places

A   apartment building

B   café

C   large store

D   library

E   museum

F   post office

G   sports centre

H   station

You now have 6 minutes to write your answers on the answer sheet.

Test 3

READING AND WRITING (60 minutes)

PART 1

QUESTIONS 1–6

For each question, choose the correct answer.

1

Toby,
Thanks for inviting me to your badminton party at the sports club next Saturday afternoon. Will I know anyone else there?
Ben

Ben wants to know

A   who is going to the party.

B   what they're going to do at the party.

C   what time the party starts.

2

Summer show
I have some great actors and dancers but still need people who play instruments.
We practise Tuesdays and Thursdays after school.
Mrs Jenkins

For the show, Mrs Jenkins is looking for

A   some better actors and dancers.

B   anyone with free time this summer.

C   students who are good at music.

3

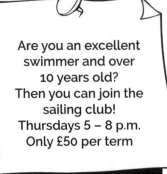

Are you an excellent swimmer and over 10 years old?
Then you can join the sailing club!
Thursdays 5 – 8 p.m.
Only £50 per term

A   New members of any age are welcome to join the club.

B   You must be able to swim to become a member of the club.

C   There is a special price for new members who join the club on Thursday.

4

Justin,
Have you still got that history book of mine? Could you let me have it back because Rob needs it for the weekend?
Sally

What should Justin do?

A   lend the book to Rob when he's finished reading it

B   return the book so that someone else can read it

C   use the book over the weekend

5

Serena,
I saw your text about Dad's birthday present, but we always get him socks! What about sunglasses? Mum can take us to get some.
Karin

A   Karin doesn't agree with Serena about what to buy their father.

B   Karin thinks their mother will have better ideas for a present.

C   Karin doesn't know what to buy her father for his birthday.

6

City Library

Library computers are for members only – ask receptionist about becoming a member.

A   You need to ask the receptionist which computers you can use.

B   Only people who work at the library can use the computers.

C   If you join the library, you can use the computers.

PART 2

QUESTIONS 7–13

For each question, choose the correct answer.

		Joshua	Dan	Chris
7	Who says his teacher helps with things other than science?	A	B	C
8	Who says his teacher is really interested in what she teaches?	A	B	C
9	Who says his teacher believes every student can be successful?	A	B	C
10	Who says he has chosen his future career because of his teacher?	A	B	C
11	Who says his teacher helped him to improve quickly?	A	B	C
12	Who says he's only ever had one science teacher at his school?	A	B	C
13	Who says his teacher is very good at drawing?	A	B	C

A great science teacher

Three teenagers talk about their science teachers.

Joshua

Mrs Philips was my science teacher when I joined my school and she still is, so I don't know what the other teachers are like. But I think Mrs Philips is amazing. Her lessons always seem to go really fast – she gives us so much great stuff to do. Even when we think something is too hard for us, she says she knows we can all do it, and she's usually right! She also shows us drawings, photos and websites to explain how things work, which I love.

Dan

I have a fantastic science teacher called Mrs Rhodes. She loves her subject – especially plants. She is able to draw wonderful pictures of them on the board, which helps us understand them. She never seems to get tired or bored when she's teaching. She takes time to get to know each student in the class so that she can help them better. I think she's the reason I want to be a science teacher one day.

Chris

In just one year, Mrs James has become my favourite teacher. Until I joined her class, I was very bad at science, but she explained things so well that I soon understood them better. My marks went up almost immediately. She's always happy to spend extra time with us at the end of lessons if we're having problems. But it isn't just teaching that makes her great. She's also interested in our lives and gives advice on how to be a better person.

PART 3

QUESTIONS 14–18

For each question, choose the correct answer.

Callie Rice – ice dancer

Growing up, I was in an ice-skating club, and my friends and I did lots of competitions. When I was 18, I entered a big one in Italy, and I came first. The prize was a job as an ice dancer in a big show. That's how my career started.

One of the things I love about the shows is the beautiful clothes. The only trouble is that sometimes they're heavy and I get very hot. Also, I have to change lots of times in one show. The people who make the clothes are very clever – it's amazing how quickly they work!

Before the show starts, we get dressed, put our skates on, and wish each other good luck. Then, while I'm waiting to go on, I like to sit quietly by myself and think about what I'm going to do. The other skaters chat together or listen to music.

In the shows, we have to dance, sing, and also speak. For me, ice dancing is fine, but I'm not an actor. I'm always a bit scared I won't remember the words. I'm not bothered about falling – it doesn't usually happen. And I really enjoy joining in with all the songs.

People always ask me if I'm tired when each show finishes, but I love skating, so I never feel that way. I love listening to the people who came to watch – so excited as they leave, talking about what they've seen. That's when I'm really happy I chose ice dancing as a career.

---

14   How did Callie's career as an ice dancer begin?

A   She won a competition.

B   She saw an advert for a job.

C   A friend invited her to join an ice show.

15   What does Callie say about the clothes she wears?

A   Some are prettier than others.

B   It's hard to skate in them.

C   Making them takes a long time.

16   What does Callie do just before each show?

A   She talks to the other skaters.

B   She checks her skates are okay.

C   She takes a moment to be alone.

17   What does Callie worry about?

A   having an accident on the ice

B   forgetting what she has to say

C   dancing and singing at the same time

18   How does Callie usually feel after a show?

A   ready for a rest

B   glad that she's finished

C   pleased about making people happy

PART 4

QUESTIONS 19–24

For each question, choose the correct answer.

Art you can eat

Yujia Hu was born in China, but moved to Milan, in Italy, when he was eight. His family have a Japanese restaurant there. When Yujia left school, he **(19)** .... a course at an art school, but he didn't complete it. **(20)** .... , he went to work in the family restaurant as a sushi chef. Sushi is a Japanese dish made of rice, with fish and vegetables.

Yujia is a big **(21)** .... of basketball, and a few years ago he **(22)** .... to start using sushi to make models of the faces of famous players. His next idea was to make little shoes, usually trainers, out of sushi. It **(23)** .... him about 30 minutes to make each shoe. Yujia doesn't serve the sushi shoes to customers at his family's restaurant, but he **(24)** .... photographs of them online.

19	**A**	got	**B**	held	**C**	began

20	**A**	Instead	**B**	Really	**C**	Maybe

21	**A**	partner	**B**	fan	**C**	member

22	**A**	believed	**B**	understood	**C**	decided

23	**A**	spends	**B**	takes	**C**	delays

24	**A**	sends	**B**	shares	**C**	joins

PART 5

QUESTIONS 25–30

For each question, write the correct answer.

Write **ONE** word for each gap.

Example:

0	*are*

From:	Jason
To:	Mum

We **(0)** .... all having a great time camping in the forest. My class has got **(25)** ....
best place on the campsite, with a great view of the mountains.

Last night, **(26)** .... rained really hard. Lots of people got wet, **(27)** .... I was
lucky my new tent stayed dry all night! I'm really glad we decided to buy it. It's much better
(28) .... my old one.

By the way, I forgot **(29)** .... tell the football coach that I'm away **(30)** .... the
moment. Can you let him know that I can't come to practice this week?

Thanks!

PART 6

QUESTION 31

Read the email from your English friend, Chris.

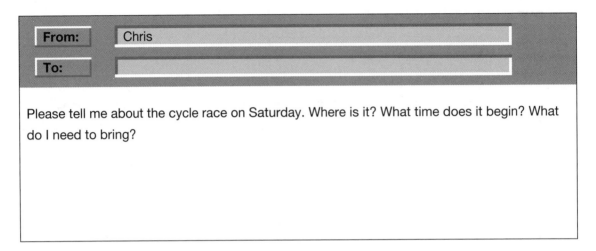

| From: | Chris |
| To: | |

Please tell me about the cycle race on Saturday. Where is it? What time does it begin? What do I need to bring?

Write an email to Chris and answer the questions.
Write **25 words** or more.

Write the email on your answer sheet.

PART 7

QUESTION 32

Look at the three pictures.

Write the story shown in the pictures.

Write **35 words** or more.

Write the story on your answer sheet.

LISTENING (approximately 30 minutes)

PART 1

QUESTIONS 1–5

For each question, choose the correct answer.

---

1   What does the boy's mother need to buy for him?

A   B   C

2   What's the girl trying to make?

A   B   C

3   What was the weather like at the weekend?

A   B   C

4   What will the boy have for lunch?

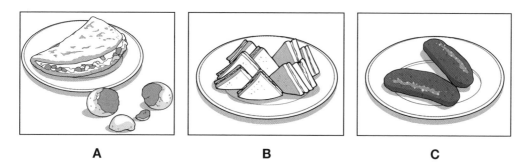

       A   **B**   **C**

5   Which subject won't they study next year?

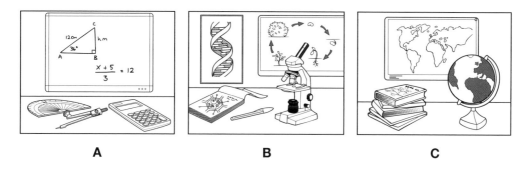

       A   **B**   **C**

PART 2

QUESTIONS 6–10

For each question, write the correct answer in the gap.
Write **one word** or a **number** or a **date** or a **time**.

You will hear a student talking to her classmates about a quiz.

School Quiz

Date: 24th September

Questions about: (6) ....

Number of people in each team: (7) ....

Prize: (8) ....

Give names to: (9) Mr ....

Time to arrive: (10) .... p.m.

PART 3

QUESTIONS 11–15

For each question, choose the correct answer.

You will hear Teresa talking to her friend Daniel about a school writing competition.

11 What has Teresa decided to write about?

    A   a place she visited

    B   a film she watched

    C   a person she knows

12 How many words do students have to write for the competition?

    A   500 or less

    B   between 500 and 1000

    C   as many as they want

13 How did Daniel feel after he finished his writing?

    A   worried

    B   excited

    C   tired

14 What's the prize for winning the competition?

    A   a laptop

    B   a tablet

    C   some books

15 Teresa thinks she is good at

    A   spelling.

    B   writing stories.

    C   describing places.

PART 4

QUESTIONS 16–20

For each question, choose the correct answer.

---

16 You will hear a boy talking to a girl about his plans for the weekend.
Who is the boy meeting?

   A his brother

   B his uncle

   C his cousin

17 You will hear a girl talking to a boy.
What's the girl surprised about?

   A how warm the weather is

   B what the boy is wearing

   C how kind her teachers were

18 You will hear a girl leaving a message for her friend Adam.
What does she want Adam to do?

   A lend her something

   B explain something to her

   C give someone a message

19 You will hear a teacher speaking to a group of pupils on a trip to a river.
What activity are they going to do?

   A walking

   B fishing

   C cycling

20 You will hear two friends talking about a film they've just watched together.
What did the girl think about the film?

   A The music was too loud.

   B The story was difficult to understand.

   C The actors didn't speak clearly enough.

PART 5

QUESTIONS 21–25

For each question, choose the correct answer.

You will hear Adam talking with a friend about the sports their friends do.
What sport does each friend do now?

Example:

0	Adam	B

Friends

21	Vicky	☐
22	Oliver	☐
23	Karen	☐
24	Mike	☐
25	Ellie	☐

Sports

A	basketball
B	cycling
C	golf
D	hockey
E	snowboarding
F	swimming
G	tennis
H	volleyball

You now have 6 minutes to write your answers on the answer sheet.

Test 4

READING AND WRITING (60 minutes)

PART 1

QUESTIONS 1–6

For each question, choose the correct answer.

1

Sebastian is asking Lisa if

A she knows where the match is taking place.

B she can lend him some equipment.

C she is free to play badminton today.

2

Dave would like Mike to

A check the bus timetable for Saturday.

B ask his father to give them a lift on Saturday.

C find out the quickest way to drive to the beach.

3

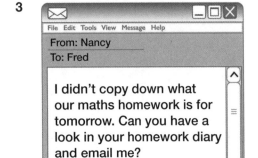

A Nancy has lost her homework diary.

B Nancy needs help with some difficult homework.

C Nancy forgot to make a note of what she needs to do.

4

School Library

From next week library will open at 8.00 and close at 5.30
(Wednesdays 8.30–4.30)

Speak to staff about booking a school laptop

A Library staff won't have much time to help you next week.

B Arrive early at the library if you would like to book a school laptop.

C The times when you can visit the library will change soon.

5

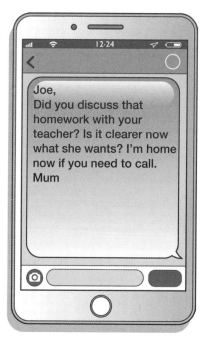

School Sports Day

(This will take place in hall instead of field if it rains – check website)
Friday, 28 September
9.00 a.m. – 3.00 p.m.
Parents and friends welcome

A If the weather is bad, we will cancel sports day.

B All students should come to the hall at 9.00 a.m. on Friday.

C Students can invite visitors to come and enjoy the day.

6

Joe,
Did you discuss that homework with your teacher? Is it clearer now what she wants? I'm home now if you need to call.
Mum

Mum is asking if Joe's teacher

A has changed his homework.

B helped him to understand his homework.

C needs to speak to her about his homework.

PART 2

QUESTIONS 7–13

For each question, choose the correct answer.

		Rhodri	Patrick	Josh
7	Who says it was easy to travel around in Rome?	A	B	C
8	Who says he felt very excited before his holiday?	A	B	C
9	Who says there was a lot of traffic in Rome?	A	B	C
10	Who says he prepared carefully for his trip?	A	B	C
11	Who said his favourite food on the trip was Italian ice cream?	A	B	C
12	Who bought some things to give as gifts?	A	B	C
13	Who took a short trip outside Rome?	A	B	C

My trip to Rome

Rhodri

I had a great time in Rome with my family. It was my first holiday outside my own country and I couldn't wait to go. I found out all I could about Rome from the library and on the internet. Knowing about the history made seeing all the old buildings, like the Colosseum, much more interesting. We were able to do lots of sightseeing because the taxis and buses and the metro were cheap and fast.

Patrick

It was really hot when I arrived at Rome airport with my parents last summer. I loved walking around famous places like the Trevi Fountain, but all the cars and buses in the city sometimes made walking difficult. I really loved the food. The Italians have a special kind of ice cream called 'gelato' which is wonderful, but the best thing I had was a pizza at a local market. I also got some great things to take back for my friends.

Josh

It was so hot when my dad and I went to Rome last year that we usually waited until after the sun went down to explore the city on foot. During the day we went to museums, shops and restaurants. The pasta there is amazing, and I had some Italian ice cream, called 'gelato', for the first time. That was the thing I liked most. After a few days in Rome, we decided to take a train into the countryside for a day. It was nice to see all the small villages and farms.

PART 3

QUESTIONS 14–18

For each question, choose the correct answer.

A wonderful year

Ben Jones talks about his year of travel before studying at university.

I always knew I wanted to spend a year travelling before university. I wanted to see the world, improve my skiing, make new friends from other countries and, more than anything, try lots of things I've never done before.

The first place I visited was France. I've always loved the French language and I wanted to study it. Then, while I was there, I became interested in French food. I took some cooking lessons at a farmhouse in the French countryside, and learned to make lots of lovely dishes.

Next, I visited Australia. My cousins live near the river in Sydney, so I had somewhere to stay. To begin with, we spent a lot of time sailing in their boat. But then I got a job in a hotel. It was great – the customers and staff were so friendly.

My last country was Japan, where I learned to become a skiing teacher. I planned to do a three-week course. But when I got there, I saw that I wasn't actually that good, so I changed to a seven-week one. The course was amazing and afterwards I got a job with a skiing company.

The other teachers were very friendly and on our days off, we did activities like snowboarding. One weekend we even did winter camping. That was quite interesting, but it was cold, so I can't say I slept well! Anyway, we're all planning to meet up soon and I can't wait.

---

14 What did Ben want to do during the year after he left school?

    A   try some different sports

    B   have some new experiences

    C   meet up with old friends

15 Why did Ben go to France?

    A   to do a French cooking course

    B   to see the French countryside

    C   to learn to speak French

16 Where did Ben live when he was in Australia?

    A   in the hotel where he worked

    B   with members of his family

    C   on a boat on the river

17 Why did Ben change his course in Japan?

    A   He heard about a better one.

    B   He knew he needed more practice.

    C   He wasn't enjoying the first one.

18 What does Ben say about winter camping?

    A   It wasn't pleasant at night.

    B   He would love to do it again soon.

    C   It was the most interesting thing he's ever done.

PART 4

QUESTIONS 19–24

For each question, choose the correct answer.

Eric Koston

Eric Koston is one of the world's best-known skateboarders. He was born in Thailand, but his family **(19)** .... to the US when he was a baby. His love of skateboarding began at the **(20)** .... of 11, when his older brother gave him a skateboard. It was an old, broken board, but he learned how to skateboard by watching other kids and then he **(21)** .... by himself every day.

Three years later, he was so good that a company that made skateboards offered him a summer **(22)** .... That's when he **(23)** .... to make skateboarding his life. Since then, Eric has **(24)** .... many international competitions, made boarding videos and starred in a skateboarding video game. Now he owns a successful company making sports shoes and clothes.

19	**A** changed	**B** moved	**C** left
20	**A** year	**B** time	**C** age
21	**A** practised	**B** taught	**C** followed
22	**A** career	**B** job	**C** work
23	**A** thought	**B** felt	**C** decided
24	**A** won	**B** taken	**C** tried

PART 5

QUESTIONS 25–30

For each question, write the correct answer.

Write **ONE** word for each gap.

Example:

0	from

Hi everyone. My name is Juan and I've joined this website because I'm looking for a
penfriend. I come **(0)** .... Mexico and I live in a town called Playa del Carmen on the
Caribbean Sea, near the city of Cancun. It's not as famous **(25)** .... Cancun but I think it
is one of **(26)** .... most beautiful places in Mexico.

Tourists come to Playa del Carmen from **(27)** .... over the world because the weather's
always warm and the food's great. **(28)** .... fact, my friends and I go to the beach
almost every day. It's brilliant!

Do you want **(29)** .... know more about Playa del Carmen? **(30)** .... you do, write
to me soon.

PART 6

QUESTION 31

Read the email from your English friend, Casey.

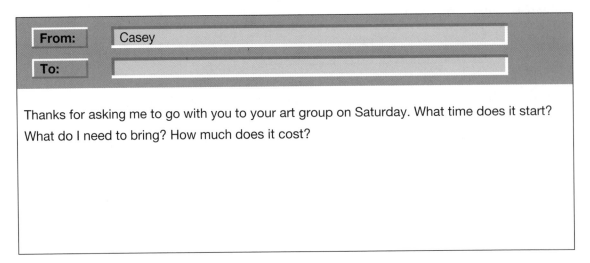

From: Casey

To:

Thanks for asking me to go with you to your art group on Saturday. What time does it start? What do I need to bring? How much does it cost?

Write an email to Casey and answer the questions.
Write **25 words** or more.

Write the email on your answer sheet.

PART 7

QUESTION 32

Look at the three pictures.

Write the story shown in the pictures.

Write **35 words** or more.

Write the story on your answer sheet.

LISTENING (approximately 30 minutes)

PART 1
QUESTIONS 1–5

For each question, choose the correct answer.

---

1 Who is the boy's sister?

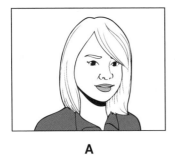  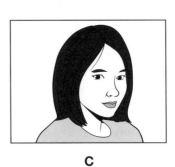

    A   **B**   **C**

2 Why didn't the girl go to the school dance?

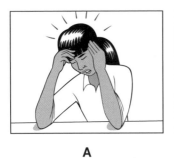  

    A   **B**   **C**

3 Where's the girl going first?

  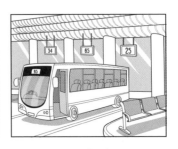

    A   **B**   **C**

4   Which programme will the two friends watch together?

A   B   C

5   Where will the girl go tomorrow?

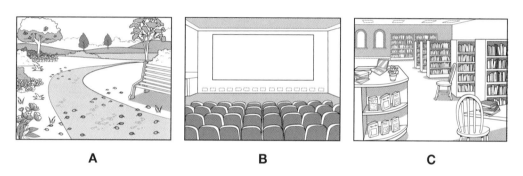

A   B   C

PART 2

QUESTIONS 6–10

For each question, write the correct answer in the gap. Write **one word** or a **number** or a **date** or a **time**.

You will hear a girl called Sophia leaving a message for her friend.

Holiday with Sophia

Time to arrive at Sophia's house:	1.45 p.m.
Name of hotel:	(6) The ....
Not available at hotel:	(7) ....
For journey, bring:	(8) ....
Weather will be:	(9) ....
Sophia's sister's phone number:	(10) ....

PART 3

QUESTIONS 11–15

For each question, choose the correct answer.

You will hear Maria talking to her friend Alex about visiting a science museum.

11 Maria went to the museum

    A   on Sunday.

    B   on Monday.

    C   on Tuesday.

12 Alex usually goes to the museum with his

    A   class.

    B   friends.

    C   family.

13 Alex usually travels to the museum

    A   by bike.

    B   by bus.

    C   on foot.

14 What did Maria prefer at the museum?

    A   talking to the guide

    B   watching a video

    C   making a model

15 In the café, Maria had

    A   a cake.

    B   an ice cream.

    C   a drink.

PART 4

QUESTIONS 16–20

For each question, choose the correct answer.

_____

16 You will hear a teacher talking to his students.
What does he tell them?

   A   They've got less work to do.

   B   They should do more exercise.

   C   They've got more time to study.

17 You will hear a girl, Emily, talking to her mum in the kitchen.
What's Emily's mum doing?

   A   making a shopping list

   B   explaining how to cook a dish

   C   deciding what they're going to eat

18 You will hear a girl talking to her friend Dan.
What job does Dan's mum do?

   A   She's a guide.

   B   She's a receptionist.

   C   She's a shop assistant.

19 You will hear a mother and daughter talking together.
What will they do today?

   A   visit the hospital

   B   go to the train station

   C   buy some stamps

20 You will hear two friends talking about something they did together at the weekend.
What did they do together?

   A   visit the countryside

   B   do a sport

   C   have a meal

PART 5

QUESTIONS 21–25

For each question, choose the correct answer.

You will hear Zara telling her friend about the presents she got for her birthday.
What present did she get from each person?

Example:

0	dad	G

People

21	mum	

22	brother	

23	grandma	

24	sister	

25	uncle	

Presents

A   backpack

B   basketball

C   book

D   bracelet

E   poster

F   scarf

G   tablet

H   tent

You now have 6 minutes to write your answers on the answer sheet.

Sample answer sheet: Reading and Writing

Draft

Cambridge Assessment
English

Candidate Name		Candidate Number	

Centre Name		Centre Number	

Examination Title		Examination Details	

Candidate Signature		Assessment Date	

Supervisor: If the candidate is ABSENT or has WITHDRAWN shade here ○

Key for Schools Reading and Writing Candidate Answer Sheet

Instructions
Use a PENCIL (B or HB).
Rub out any answer you want to change with an eraser.

For Parts 1, 2, 3 and 4:
Mark ONE letter for each answer.
For example: If you think A is the right answer to
the question, mark your answer sheet like this:

For Part 5:
Write your answers clearly in the spaces next
to the numbers (25 to 30) like this:

Write your answers in CAPITAL LETTERS.

Part 1

	A	B	C
1	○	○	○
2	○	○	○
3	○	○	○
4	○	○	○
5	○	○	○
6	○	○	○

Part 2

	A	B	C
7	○	○	○
8	○	○	○
9	○	○	○
10	○	○	○
11	○	○	○
12	○	○	○
13	○	○	○

Part 3

	A	B	C
14	○	○	○
15	○	○	○
16	○	○	○
17	○	○	○
18	○	○	○

Part 4

	A	B	C
19	○	○	○
20	○	○	○
21	○	○	○
22	○	○	○
23	○	○	○
24	○	○	○

Part 5

		Do not write below here
25		25 1 ○ 0 ○
26		26 1 ○ 0 ○
27		27 1 ○ 0 ○

		Do not write below here
28		28 1 ○ 0 ○
29		29 1 ○ 0 ○
30		30 1 ○ 0 ○

Put your answers to Writing Parts 6 and 7 on the separate Answer Sheet

Draft

Draft

Cambridge Assessment
English

Candidate Name		**Candidate Number**	
Centre Name		**Centre Number**	
Examination Title		**Examination Details**	
Candidate Signature		**Assessment Date**	

Supervisor: If the candidate is ABSENT or has WITHDRAWN shade here ○

Key for Schools Writing

Candidate Answer Sheet for Parts 6 and 7

INSTRUCTIONS TO CANDIDATES

Make sure that your name and candidate number are on this sheet.

Write your answers to Writing Parts 6 and 7 on the other side of this sheet.

Use a pencil.

You **must** write within the grey lines.

Do **not** write on the bar codes.

Draft

Sample answer sheet: Reading and Writing

Draft

Part 6: Write your answer below.

Part 7: Write your answer below.

Examiner's Use Only

Part 6	C	O	L

Part 7	C	O	L

Draft

 　Photocopiable

Draft

OFFICE USE ONLY - DO NOT WRITE OR MAKE ANY MARK ABOVE THIS LINE   Page 1 of 1

Cambridge Assessment English

Candidate Name		Candidate Number	
Centre Name		Centre Number	
Examination Title		Examination Details	
Candidate Signature		Assessment Date	

Supervisor: If the candidate is ABSENT or has WITHDRAWN shade here ○

Key for Schools Listening Candidate Answer Sheet

Instructions
Use a PENCIL (B or HB).
Rub out any answer you want to change with an eraser.

For Parts 1, 3, 4 and 5:
Mark ONE letter for each answer.
For example: If you think A is the right answer to the question, mark your answer sheet like this:

For Part 2:
Write your answers clearly in the spaces next to the numbers (6 to 10) like this:

Write your answers in CAPITAL LETTERS.

Part 1
1 A B C
2 A B C
3 A B C
4 A B C
5 A B C

Part 2
6 — 6 1 0
7 — 7 1 0
8 — 8 1 0
9 — 9 1 0
10 — 10 1 0

Part 3
11 A B C
12 A B C
13 A B C
14 A B C
15 A B C

Part 4
16 A B C
17 A B C
18 A B C
19 A B C
20 A B C

Part 5
21 A B C D E F G H
22 A B C D E F G H
23 A B C D E F G H
24 A B C D E F G H
25 A B C D E F G H

OFFICE USE ONLY - DO NOT WRITE OR MAKE ANY MARK BELOW THIS LINE   Page 1 of 1
Draft

© UCLES 2019 Photocopiable   75

Acknowledgements

The authors and publishers acknowledge the following sources of copyright material and are grateful for the permissions granted. While every effort has been made, it has not always been possible to identify the sources of all the material used, or to trace all copyright holders. If any omissions are brought to our notice, we will be happy to include the appropriate acknowledgements on reprinting and in the next update to the digital edition, as applicable.

Key: T = Test, RW = Reading & Writing, P = Part.

Text

T3 P4: courtesy of Yujia Hu. Reproduced with kind permission.

Photographs

All the photographs are sourced from Getty Images.

T1 RW P2: ajr_images/iStock/Getty Images Plus; Image Source; DGLimages/iStock/Getty Images Plus;
T2 RW P2: Juanmonino/iStock/Getty Images Plus; Gary John Norman/DigitalVision; MaFelipe/E+;
T3 RW P2: Jennifer Kelly Photography/Moment Open; drbimages/E+; Priscilla Gragg/Blend Images;
T3 RW P4: Nattapol Poonpiriya/EyeEm;
T4 RW P2: Juan Silva/Photodisc; SolStock/iStock/Getty Images Plus; smailciydem/iStock/Getty Images Plus.

Typeset by QBS Learning.

Audio production by Real Deal Productions and dsound recording Ltd.

Visual materials for the Speaking test

Test 1
Do you like these different things to wear?

Test 2

Do you like these different outdoor activities?

Test 3

Do you like these different fun activities?

Test 4
Do you like these different school subjects?